THE IMPERATIVE OF UTU/UBUNTU IN AFRICANA SCHOLARSHIP

Mîcere Gîthae Mũgo

Published by Daraja Press
https://darajapress.com

ISBN 9781990263248

Library and Archives Canada Cataloguing in Publication
Title: The imperative of Utu/Ubuntu in Africana scholarship / by Micere Githae Mugo.
Names: Mugo, Micere Githae, author.
Description: Series statement: Thinking freedom | Includes bibliographical references.
Identifiers: Canadiana 20210246138 | ISBN 9781990263248 (softcover)
Subjects: LCSH: Ubuntu (Philosophy) | LCSH: Learning and scholarship.
Classification: LCC B5315.U28 M84 2021 | DDC 199/.68—dc23

CONTENTS

ACKNOWLEDGEMENTS

I wish to thank Prof. N'Dri Assie-Lumumba and the planning committee of Africana Studies and Research Center's 50th anniversary celebration for proposing my name as the keynote speaker on this very special occasion. It is a unique honor and privilege, for, as I will elaborate momentarily, this is no ordinary occasion.

For now, please allow me to say something about my colleague and sister, Professor N'Dri Assie-Lumumba, who has coordinated and chaired the committee planning for this event. Sister N'Dri, as I refer to her, is not just a prolific scholar and internationally celebrated intellectual, but a woman of unthwarted will. She is famous and I have no doubt, notorious in the eyes of her detractors, for her persistence, insistence, consistency and commitment to any task that she undertakes. Where I come from, people would, metaphorically, argue that she will make a stone yield water. Permit me to elaborate. At the time Sister N'Dri approached me to speak last year, this stone that you see before you today had firmly halted all non-emergency travel, regular speaking engagements, conferences and so on...due to health challenges. The only agenda items that remained solidly on my schedule were: work on Njeri's Global Children Foundation;[1] participation in selected

1 When my younger daughter, Njeri Kũi, passed away on October 4, 2012, following a brief, intensive and sheroic battle with ovarian cancer, Mũmbi and I established a foundation in her memory. Family members and friends contributed generously to ensure the project took off; but since then, Mũmbi and I have had to provide funding for the foundation which is still active today. Since 2013, we have offered the Njeri Global Children Award annually to "underserved," gifted students (mainly in Kenyan schools), who would have otherwise dropped out of school due to inability to pay fees. To date, 24 such children have been beneficiaries. Njeri believed that: *"In the deepest of places within the person of each child, there is a kernel of genius just sitting there waiting to be let loose to enter the world of learning, discovery, self-discovery, collective discovery and celebration of the multifarious gifts that life so generously gives,"* quoted from her doctoral dissertation proposal. In her view, impoverishment and other forms of social injustice sabotage the blooming of this "kernel of genius." Thus, Njeri's ultimate vision was to establish schools for underserved children, internationally, with a curriculum that focused on bringing out the repressed "kernel of genius" in every child.

community organizations, and community activism in general. Thus, when Sister N'Dri explained that the event was in celebration of Africana's 50th anniversary, I knew this was no ordinary occasion and promptly said "yes." So, behold here before you, the metaphorical stone that Professor Assie-Lumumba made to yield water. Thank you very much, Sister N'Dri. We celebrate you as a teacher, scholar and intellectual. We salute you for your total commitment to Black Studies, Gender and Women's Studies; and global education in general. We commend you for the special love and dedication you have shown towards the Africana Studies and Research Center at Cornell University for over thirty years.

Professor Olufemi Taiwo, Director of Africana Studies, thank you for the warmth and validation of your invitation. Your letter was truly touching in its appreciation of what I have, humbly, contributed as an educator. With your permission, I would like to quote the portion in which you, graciously, thanked me for "*...the advancement of Black Studies, the training of its graduates, the fostering of communities...the continuing task of ensuring that peoples of African descent enrich all humanity and receive their due recognition for so doing. Your work both in the motherland continent and here in the Diaspora has been a source of illumination, encouragement and, we must not forget, enjoyment for all of us who have been privileged to read, watch, and hear them.*"

Mr. Director, I now definitely know who to go to for my next letter of reference. Seriously, thank you very much, Professor Taiwo, for these humbling words.

To all who have contributed towards my coming here, I offer a resounding "thank you."

To my esteemed colleagues at Africana, I respect and salute each one of you for your intellectual guardianship of this critical site of knowledge – the parent of all Black Studies in the United States of America. Thank you for heeding Assata Shakur, who implores the benefactors and benefactresses of every her/historical struggle to carry on "the tradition:"

Through the lies and sell-outs.
Through mistakes and madness.
Through pain and hunger and frustration,
We carried it on.

Carried on the tradition.
Carried a strong tradition
Carried a proud tradition
Carried on a Black tradition
Carry it on.

Pass it down to the children.
Pass it down.
Carry it on now.
Carry it on
TO FREEDOM[2]

To all my dear relatives and friends who have joined us from abroad, nationally and locally, I extend a very warm welcome to you and deep appreciation for your support. Just from the acceptances that I had received to my personal invitation as of yesterday, I believe we have an international audience from the following countries, alphabetically: Britain; Canada; Kenya; South Africa; Sweden; U.S.A., and Zimbabwe. A special "thank you" to those living in time zones where it is already late in the night. I cannot thank you enough for sacrificing your sleep and staying up late to be with us. I greatly value your generosity and solidarity.

Lastly, allow me, as is my habit, to thank my daughter, friend, sister and comrade, Mũmbi wa Mũgo, Senior Manager with Accenture Inc. Mũmbi normally keeps long working days to keep her demanding load of work under control and so by joining us in this celebration, she will probably be still laboring late

2˜Assata Shakur, "The Tradition," in *Assata – An Autobiography.* Chicago: Lawrence Hill Books, 1987, pp. 264-5.

in the night, long after I have gone to bed. Hopefully, my snores will not be too loud to disturb her as she struggles to concentrate on what she is doing. Seriously, I ask you: what more could a parent ask of a daughter? Thank you so, so much, Mũmbi.

Special Dedication

I dedicate this "lecture" to my late daughter and Mũmbi's younger sister, Njeri Kũi Gĩthae-Mũgo, whom we lost to ovarian cancer on October 4, 2012. At the time of her passage, she had just graduated from Edinburgh University with an MSc in Childhood Education and was teaching in China with a view to obtaining practical field experience before embarking on a PhD at either Harvard, or Columbia, or Vanderbilt. Her intellectual growth was not just amazing and exciting to watch, but its firm rootedness in utu/ubuntu[3] was quite rare in a young scholar. Njeri is an alumna of the Africana Studies and Research Center, Cornell University, where she did her MPS on graduating from Smith College with a B.A. and a Five College Area Associates Certificate in African Studies. I believe that she is with us today reminding us that utu/ubuntu are imperative if the work we do is to change the world for the better. In this regard, I wish to acknowledge the contribution of Africana Studies and Research Center at Cornell to Njeri's intellectual growth. My family's special thanks go to Professor James Turner, the founding director of ASRC and the chair of Njeri's MPS degree committee; Professor Assie-Lumumba, member of the committee and Professor Anne Adams, her general mentor at AS&RS, for their guidance and nurturing.

This publication is an expanded, edited and annotated version of a shorter online lecture entitled *The imperative of Utu/Ubuntu in scholarship if Africana studies and research are to be celebrated as liberated zones in academia*, which I delivered as the keynote address at the Africana Studies and Research Center,

3 The bottom of Njeri's email page had a quotation from Archbishop Desmond Tutu, which I will cite fully later.

Cornell University's 50th Anniversary Celebration, on Wednesday, May 5, 2021. The original version of the paper was delivered as a public lecture at the University of Montana on September 23, 2019, under the title, "I am because we are: the imperative of Utu/Ubuntu in transformational scholarship." An abridged version of it, under the same title, was delivered to Professor Horace Campbell's Pan African Studies Program's graduate class, in the Department of African American Studies, at Syracuse University, on November 4, 2019.

The publication is, thus, the final product of a prolonged "project" that attempts to explore ways of highlighting Africana indigenous knowledges and proposes possible theoretical, methodological and scholarly alternative approaches that could infuse utu/ubuntu into Africana teaching, research and scholarship in general. I am indebted to Firoze Manji and Daraja Press for inviting me to publish the paper with the aim of reaching a wider audience.

AFRICAN ORATURE MODE OF DELIVERY

For nearly three decades now, I have striven to infuse my scholarship, including creative writing and oral/verbal presentations, with African orature[4] ethics and aesthetics, as well as their paradigms and theoretical formulations. This has partly been an attempt to respond to Amilcar Cabral's call to Africa's colonized elite and members of the intelligentsia to "return to the source."[5] However, it has also been my conscious effort to affirm African indigenous knowledges as valid and critical sites for academic engagement. I describe this ongoing engagement as 'excavating the gold mines of African indigenous knowledges.' As someone who is primarily grounded in the creative arts, the task has involved learning from orate[6] specialists and practitioners in/of African oracy, and of orature in particular. In African orature, discourse is both conversational and interactive. The speaker

4 Note: I insist on using the term *orature* (meaning verbal art, or the art of the spoken word) as opposed to Oral literature, a term that, in my view, begs the question. I am in agreement with the case that Pio Zirimu and Austin Bukenya make in their seminal piece on "Oracy as a Skill and as a Tool for African Development," in *The Arts and Civilizations of Black and African Peoples*, Vol 10; Eds. Joseph Okpaku et al; New York: Third Press/Joseph Okpaku Publishing Company Inc., 1986. Namely: lit-e-ra-ture is the written word; while ora-ture is the spoken word. I have further argued that to name Orature, "Oral literature," is to relegate orature to the role of an adjective and thus privilege and elevate "literature" to be the subject. It is no wonder that a lot of literary critics have made the error of analyzing Orature in literary terms, dismissing the validity of orature's ethics and aesthetics when they do not conform to those of the written word. I say: Orature is orature, period. It is a unique heritage in its own right. Thus, whereas there might be some overlapping and similarities in conceptualizing the two heritages – the written and the spoken—they are two distinct "traditions," each one having specific ethics and aesthetics of its own.

5 Reference to Amilcar Cabral's essay, "National Liberation and Culture," in *Return to the Source: Selected Speeches of Amilcar Cabral*, ed. African Information Service, New York: Monthly Press, 1973, pp. 39-56.

6 Zirimu's and Bukenya's coinage to describe experts who are trained in and well-versed in oracy (the ability to speak well). They are also, usually, specialists in orature, or verbal art (the artistry of the spoken/performed word, unfolded through genres such as legends and myths; stories; drama; theatre; poetry, proverbs, riddles etc.) According to Zirimu and Bukenya, orature is oracy in action; it is the highest expression and manifestation of oracy.

considers her/his audience fellow-travelers and essential participants in the narrative s/he is unfolding. To ensure this, s/he will pause from time to time and either ask them a question, or invite their involvement, usually by using what Black art calls "call and response," or by building into the spoken text, refrains (repeated statements) that reinforce the theme of her/his presentation. Unfortunately, these techniques will not work in a virtually delivered presentation.

LIBERATED ACADEMIC ZONES

My revered audience, today's 50th anniversary celebration is much, much more than an Africana Studies at Cornell University event. It symbolizes and marks a herstorical/historical event that is bigger than ASRC. It symbolizes the moment at the height of the Civil Rights Movement and activism, when Black communities in America, supported by progressive activists in the US as well as in the entire world, challenged white supremacist ethos. It symbolizes the creation of Black studies as liberated zones in White-centered academia.

Let us poetize these activists on this 50th anniversary celebration at Africana, Cornell, where:

- The liberators organized resistance, protests and demonstrations under extremely dangerous conditions.
- They denounced racism and rebelled against the negation of Black people.
- They decried the abuse of human rights and attempted-erasure of dominated communities, especially people of African origin.
- They demanded recognition as human beings: equals and makers of her/history.
- *They created liberated academic zones!*

- Yes, progressive students and Black scholars, supported by those who stood in solidarity with them, rose up and joined the Civil Rights Movement.
- These intellectuals rejected intellectual isolationism and located themselves within their Black communities.

- They challenged the discrimination and exclusivity of all-White and predominantly-White institutions, rigorously interrogating the mission behind their White-centered curricula in education.
- These students and scholars exploded the false myth that knowledge was the given monopoly of dominating White cultures.
- *They created liberated academic zones!*
- *This is why and how Black Studies as an academic field was born. This why and how the Africana Studies and Research Center at Cornell University was born. Today, in celebrating Africana as a liberated zone, let us say Asé!*

Fellow-travelers, to purposefully repeat myself: this celebration symbolizes that moment when activists, students and scholars of African/Black origin, plus their progressive counterparts, vowed to put a full stop to the arrogant false myths that Black studies were devoid of any academic content. Nay, could never be seriously considered sites of learned intellectual inquiry. They were altogether irrelevant to education and human "civilization." This celebration reminds us of that critical moment when communities of activists, students and Africana scholars intervened and denounced this attempted erasure by imperialists. They derided the historical negation of their cultural heritages and the distortion of who they and their people were. ...They riled and rebelled against the imperialist doctrine that Aimé Césaire[7] once identified as the "thingification" of dominated people, their personhood and their cultures.

Our predecessors rose up and vowed to name themselves on their own terms. They claimed ownership of their heritages and seized back Africana's sites of knowledge abducted by colonizers who had declared themselves experts in the study of Africa. They

7 Aimé Césaire, *Discourse on Colonialism*, Paris: Présence Africaine, 1955.

even taught African indigenous languages as carriers of African culture and civilization. The liberators created liberated zones on white and predominantly white campuses... And then, and THEN, they demarcated and carved spaces of their own – right in the belly of the beast, as the ancient wise ones would say.

Our predecessors named these liberated zones variously: Africana Studies; African American Studies; Afro-American Studies; Black Studies; Africology, etc. Whatever the naming or emphasis of a particular liberated zone, however, the umbrella theme and resounding motif were the same: the establishment of interdisciplinary programs in Black studies, focusing on the African continent and its global diaspora. To wit, the vision was Pan Africanist and Black community-centered, but it was never exclusive of other cultures.

Fellow celebrants, this is the context within which the Africana Studies and Research Center at Cornell was born in 1969. Who does not know about this herstorical and historical epic in academia? Listen as we revisit, Sankofa-visioned, the scene of Africana's birth. Following the s/hero/ic student take-over of Willard Straight Hall (Cornell University's administrative building), the walls of the fort collapsed under activist-pressure and the gates opened for Black people, reluctantly. Students of color trickled in and colored the campus's whiteness... forever... Therefore, let us never lose sight of the critical role played by students (mainly Black, but supported by progressive white mates). Let us never forget that Black communities were at the heart of these struggles. Let us forever remember the resolute and visionary leadership of Emeritus Professor James Turner, the founding Director of Africana Studies and Research Center – an Africana intellectual warrior with a razor-sharp vision, always located in the Black community.

UTU AND UBUNTU

I will begin with defining *Utu/Ubuntu* so that we have a common point of departure. After defining the operational terms, I will address the question of ownership of knowledge, its production, dissemination and custodianship. The heart of my argument is that knowledge and scholarship can either be colonizing, alienating and enslaving; or alternatively, they can be conscientizing, humanizing and liberating, creating new human beings with the agency to transform the world for the better.[8] The second option constitutes what I call *utu/ubuntu rooted-scholarship,* which should, in my view, define Africana studies, research and scholarship, if they are to be celebrated as liberated zones in academia.

What do we mean by *Utu/Ubuntu?* Here, I will plagiarize myself and either heavily reference, or extensively quote from the public lecture that birthed this publication and that was delivered at the University of Montana in September 2019, under the title, "I am because we are: the imperative of *Utu/Ubuntu* in transformational scholarship."

The late Dr. John Mbiti, one of my favorite undergraduate professors who taught me Greek and Hebrew – languages I have long forgotten! – at Makerere University in the early sixties, was also an expert in African philosophy and traditional religions, both of which I studied under him. I will forever be indebted to him for having introduced me to the ancient communal world

8 General reference to Mĩcere Gĩthae Mũgo, "Introduction," *Writing and Speaking From the Heart of My Mind*, Trenton, N.J.: Africa World Press, 2012.

view of African people, their philosophical formulations and their indigenous religious beliefs. I hope some of you have read his work and in particular, *African Religions and Philosophy*.[9] In this seminal publication, the late Professor Mbiti notes that although there is a danger in generalizing on African cultures and beliefs considering how numerous and diversified, they are, nonetheless an argument can be made that they share a basic philosophy of life. He summarizes this basic philosophy of life as: "I am because you are and since you are, therefore I am." Orature, or verbal art, in many African societies reflects this shared worldview. A perfect example is a greeting among the Shona people of Zimbabwe which I have cited so often and for so many years that I am thankful, as well as very lucky, it is not patented. In loose translation, the exchange goes something like this:

The originator of the greeting: "How are you? Are you well?"
The respondent: "I am only well, if you too are well."

In other words, the welfare of one person is tied to the well-being of the other. Moreover, as the prolonged greeting unfolds, it becomes evident that the wellness of the individuals who are exchanging the greetings equally depend upon the wellness of their families, their extended families and their entire communities. In some African societies, the greetings become so elaborate and elongated that the enquiries even seek to know how the farms, crops, cows, goats, chickens, etc. are doing! Trust me, this is not a part of my oracy hyperbole technique. It happens in real life and in real time. So, what is the "moral of the story?" Africana scholars need to find out how to incorporate this collective and connective perception of life into their scholarship.

To wit: *I am because you are and since you are, therefore I am.*

Let us look more closely at *utu* as a concept.

9 John Mbiti, *African Religions and Philosophy*, New York: Doubleday, 1970.

Utu is a Kiswahili term meaning,*"hali ya mtu kuwa na tabia ya kibinadamu."* I am sure nobody in this international audience had any problem understanding that. Right? Just in case anyone is too shy to confess, the approximate translation of the definition into English would be: "The state of a person who has the habit of being human." Talk of African oracy's paradoxical statements! Simply and in plain language, *utu* is the capacity to exhibit behavior that is humane.

Utu is based on the philosophy that the soul is paramount and that losing it is worse than losing all one's material wealth. It is based on the philosophy that to be whole and to define one's personhood and one's humanity, the human physical form is inadequate. In other words, one's soul and inner being are the cores that define personhood – not physical, or material manifestations alone. To purposefully reiterate: having wealth – however gratifying this might be – while being spiritually poor, is a reduction of one's "personhood."

It is, therefore, imperative that as scholars of Africana studies and research, we should celebrate *Utu* by affirming the essence of humanity in what we do.

The other absolutely critical quality in *utu* is the ability to connect one's humanity to that of others.[10] I purposefully repeat: *Utu* draws from the philosophical well of understanding that John Mbiti expounds in the worldview of indigenous communal African societies. "I am because you are and since you are therefore I am." It is with this understanding that Black studies refuted the notion of exceptionalism that viewed the intelligentsia as a special clique, nay, as the chosen ones that lived above

10 In a monograph that has become a wide source of reference in African Philosophy and theorizing, I have propounded an original Orature theory, known as "The Onion Structure Theory." Refer to Mĩcere Gĩthae Mũgo, *African Orature and Human Rights*, Monograph Series, No. 13, ISAS, Roma: Lesotho, Institute of African Studies, National University of Lesotho, 1991. The theoretical invention propounds an African Orature theory, named "The Onion Structure Theory," that demonstrates the African philosophy of life's inter-relatedness and inter-connectedness as well as its affirmation of Human Rights. The research for this paper was funded by the Ford Foundation as a part of its project on Africa's indigenous contribution to Human Rights.

their communities in towers of elitism. It is for this reason that Black studies insisted on not just being a part of Black communities, but as being one with them. It is for this reason that progressive Black intellectuals not only identified with their communities, but dedicated their work to the affirmation of their people's identities, along with their heritages. It is for this reason that Black studies and research should/must not only humanize their dehumanized peoples, but seek to humanize humanity at large. This is why and how Black Studies as an academic field was born. This is why and how the Africana Studies and Research Center at Cornell University was born.

Now, is there a difference between *utu* and *ubuntu*? Not really. *Utu* (Kiswahili) and *Ubuntu* (Zulu) conceptually mean the same thing. Within the Southern African context, it is Archbishop Desmond Tutu who popularized the philosophy of *ubuntu.* But, as I have already indicated, most African societies have always had the same basic philosophy, even though it may be called something different and even be articulated differently.

Regarding *ubuntu* as articulated by Archbishop Desmond Tutu, my late daughter and Mũmbi's younger sister, Njeri Kũi Gĩthae-Mũgo, had a definitive quotation at the bottom of her email that summarizes the philosophy as popularized by the Archbishop. I quote:

> *It is the essence of being human. It speaks of the fact that my humanity is caught up and is inextricably bound up in yours. I am human because I belong. It speaks about wholeness, it speaks about compassion. A person with Ubuntu is welcoming, hospitable, warm and generous, willing to share. Such people are open and available to others, willing to be vulnerable, affirming of others, do not feel threatened that others are able and good, for they have a proper self-assurance that comes from knowing that they belong in a greater whole. They know that they are diminished*

> *when others are humiliated, diminished when others are oppressed, diminished when others are treated as if they were less than who they are. The quality of Ubuntu gives people resilience, enabling them to survive and emerge still human despite all efforts to dehumanize them.*
>
> — South African Nobel Laureate Archbishop Desmond Tutu

Rhetorical question: to what extent do our studies, research and scholarship reflect these qualities of *ubuntu*?

KNOWLEDGE: OWNERSHIP AND PRODUCTION

We now move to the question of knowledge, ownership of knowledge and production of knowledge.

The critical and irrefutable fact that we need to grasp here is that it is the vocation of all human beings to produce knowledge. At the most basic level, people do this as they relate to their surroundings and to each other in order to provide themselves with basic needs in life, namely: food, clothing and shelter. However, they go beyond this by using their minds and imagination to also embark on a deliberate journey, throughout life, to understand the world around them. Curiosity drives them to search and sound the dimensions of life with a view to unravel the unknown and to produce new knowledge. I repeat: the production of knowledge is the vocation of all human beings and of all cultures. Thus, the arrogance on the part of dominating, colonizing and imperialist cultures in not only claiming, but declaring, that they have a monopoly of knowledge, is nothing short of intellectual arrogance, dictatorship and downright imperialism. It is *the* story/fiction of conquest and empire building. It is the lie behind the dehumanization of the conquered. It is the attempted erasure of the knowledges, heritages and ultimately, the entire cultures of the dominated. For, let us bury the big lie once and for all: there is no such thing as a *one and only* system, or a *one and only* site of knowledge. Knowledge is embodied in multiple/multifarious systems, cultures and sites that thrive through interaction and exchange with each other. Sadly, colonizing and dominating cultures have failed to understand/accept this basic fact. Instead, they have imposed an imperialistic and monopolistic view and myth that depicts knowledge as the prerogative of Whites – and with tragic consequences over the course of history.

Rhetorical question: to what extent do our Africana studies, research and scholarship efforts challenge the imperialist notion of a "one and only system/site of knowledge?"

The armed and political liberation struggles of colonially invaded and occupied lands happened at a great cost: people were killed and/or maimed; their lands were forcefully taken; entire cultures were obliterated; communities were subjected to servitude, etc. The scars incurred on patriots who were often innocent people – including children – are inestimable. The long-term assault on the minds and souls of the survivors remains a trauma difficult to recover from. To be sure, the permanent damage that was caused centuries back, persists – with the debilitating effect of a prolonged hangover, hanging over generations upon generations. To achieve complete conquest of the invaded, the dominators directed their missiles not just at the bodies, but at the minds and souls of those that they colonized. This is the process that has been described by many critics of colonialism as "zombification:" the erasure of the "personhood" of the colonized, creating a "tabula rasa" on which the colonizer could write whatever he wanted. It is the process of bleaching and whitening the minds, souls and cultures of the conquered. This abuse and torture of the "captives" were a part of the colonizing mission, and it remains one of imperialism's objectives today. Thus, what I once called "the battle of the mind"[11] in the 1980s remains a reality today. It is, therefore, the imperative duty on the part of all Africana scholars to plant themselves at the heart of the struggle if we are to create liberated zones in academia.

11 Mĩcere Gĩthae Mũgo, "Battle of the Mind," UFAHAMU, California: UCLA Press, 1983.

To elaborate the point I am making, allow me to give an illustration.

Many of you will, no doubt, know the tragic story in a documentary titled *In the White Man's Image*, a source that I have cited in many of my publications. The story tells of how an American colonial educator named Richard Pratt experimented on First Nations children in an effort to acculturate and assimilate them into White culture. He forcefully, or stealthily, uprooted them from their homes and then put them in the "Carlisle School for Indians," which he had established at Carlisle, Pennsylvania, in 1879. The motto of the school was: "Kill the Indian and save the man." To do this, Pratt actively 'beat the Indian out of the children,' so to speak, to the extent of shaving their hair and restyling it in white-fashion. He put the young "captives" in uniform and drilled them like a military unit. He forbade them to speak in their languages and completely cut them off from their families, homes and cultures. Those who spoke in their mother tongues had their mouths washed in lye soap, among other forms of punishment. In this attempted cloning of Whites out of First Nations children, human collateral was immense. At least two hundred of the "captives" died of infectious diseases; others committed suicide and approximately, 20% of then ran away. Only 8% graduated from Pratt's cloning lab.

That miserable 8% "success" rate, forgive the sarcasm, nonetheless were a major loss for First Nations peoples. Having survived genocide when they were initially invaded and their lands taken, First Nations peoples were witnessing their children being subjected to new forms of genocide: the genocide of the mind and of culture. As we can well imagine, most of that 8% of the graduating class not only had their minds "captured" though brainwashing and imposed amnesia. They had been converted into colonial soldiers and collaborators: young citizens at war with their people, their cultures and ultimately, themselves. Colonial education had robbed them of their history/herstory;

their tongues and their voices. Having been torn away from their roots, the assimilated had lost contact with their communities and most tragic of all, as already intimated, they had forgotten their languages. So, when they eventually returned home, they could not communicate with their people. They became strangers in their own homes and lands. To escalate the tragedy, they had become strangers to themselves as well. Tragic. It is for this reason that we must never totalize knowledge as a process because depending on how and why it is imparted, knowledge can be destructive and enslaving, just as it can, alternatively, be constructive and liberating.

Fortunately, dialectically and historically, the more domination and oppression seek to silence their intended victims, the more the survivors learn to resist. At Carlisle, some of the 20% of the captives that escaped, plus a few from among the 8% who graduated, became rebels against colonialism. They staged uprisings and organized their communities to resist colonial occupation and domination/oppression against their people. In other words, they strove to turn First Nations' reservations into liberated zones. These struggles and those of the Civil Rights period compel all scholars of Black studies to ceaselessly resist domination if the dream of *utu/ubuntu-centered* transformational education is to be realized.

"Kill the Indian and save the man," declared Pratt, the self-appointed civilizer of First Nations People in America. *Utu/ubuntu* would say to this colonial killer-educator: "By killing the Indian you killed yourself as a human being." *Utu/ubuntu-centered* knowledge would never seek to either silence or conquer the learner, for, one of its objectives is to explode what I call "negative silences" in life. It seeks to "unsilence" the silenced and to liberate them from everything that would inhibit their total human growth. *Utu/Ubuntu-centered* knowledge transforms them from victims into agents endowed with the necessary determination, creativity and visionariness to transform the world into a better habitat for every human being. To achieve this, *utu/ubuntu* transformational scholarship should promote respect, tolerance, understanding and dialogue by inviting the world's myriad and diverse cultures to come together at a metaphorical round table to share and exchange ideas for each other's enrichment; for each other's human affirmation and growth.

Founders and advocates of Africana studies fully understood the baggage and historical crimes that accompanied the White "civilizing mission." Unfortunately, time does not allow for a detailed examination of these false imperialist sites of education and knowledge-production for conquest and domination. So, a few examples will have to suffice.

We speak of the so-called "Civilizing mission to Africa," stretching from the fifteenth to the twentieth century, that fathered and birthed false theories regarding the superiority of Whites and Whiteness versus racist notions about the inhumanity of the colonized, particularly Black/African peoples, whom they dubbed "uncivilized heathens." In other words, the so-called "Christian Civilization" era that is celebrated as an achievement in White history, produced, for the colonized, enslaving education, knowledge and religious ideas that justified such evils as (not in any historical order): slavery; colonization; occupation; eugenics; genocide; militarization; appropriation of conquered people's lands; ruthless empire building escapades and many more. In the U.S. White academy, eugenics was widely accepted as a university course. Reportedly, by '1928, there were 376 separate university courses in some of the United States' leading schools, enrolling more than 20,000 students! All of these schools included eugenics in their curriculum.' This is why Black Studies as an academic field was born.

We speak of **Sara Baartman** (1770s–29 December 1815), a South African Khoikhoi woman who was captured from South Africa and exhibited, along with a country-mate, as "freak show attractions in Europe under the name of "Hottentot Venus" because they had unusually large buttocks that their captors considered as untypical of human beings. Their captors thus objectified them by treating them as mere exotic, non-human creatures ripe for entertainment and proceeded to make huge profits at the cost of the women's humanity. The result of these so-called "educational exhibitions" was not just gross abuse of human rights and humiliation of the women; but an example of perverted racism that hid behind "education" to rationalize the dehumanization of "the other" while robbing them of their birth right and dignity as fellow-members of the human race. Sara Baartman died in Paris on 29 December 1815 around the age 40, "of an undetermined inflammatory ailment, possibly smallpox. Other sources suggest that she contracted syphilis, or pneumonia" (https://bit.ly/3z8Puwj). Following years of negotiation, her remains were finally returned to South Africa in 2002, during Nelson Mandela's presidency.

We speak of **Ota Benga** (c.1883-1916), a Mbuti people small man from what is the Congo today. Ota Benga was similarly captured from the Congo by slave traders who sold him to Samuel Philips Verner, a colonial White American missionary-cum-anthropologist-cum businessman, who then transported his "property" to the United States to be exhibited as a "pigmy." Ota Benga 'was widely featured at anthropological exhibits, including at the Louisiana Purchase Exposition in St. Louis, Missouri, in 1904; and in a human zoo exhibit in 1906 at the Bronx Zoo' (https://en.wikipedia.org/wiki/Ota_Benga). Ultimately, Ota Benga could no longer stomach the loneliness, racism, humiliation and dehumanization he was experiencing in America. He fell into a depression, and committed suicide in 1916. The book about this Congolese small man is a must read for anyone who is interested in understanding the contestations behind production and ownership of knowledge; who produces it; how they produce it; who owns it and above all, for whose benefit, or at the cost of whom/what.

We speak of what happened in Hiroshima when an atomic bomb was dropped on Japan by the United States of America and five days later, another one on the city of Nagasaki, Japan. We ask: how, in the name of human development, do we assess the "value" of the content of the kind of knowledge that went into the making of the atomic bombs that were dropped on Hiroshima and Nagasaki? Was this knowledge for the liberation and affirmation of humanity?

We speak of the research work of Josef Mengele on separating identical twins to determine whether 'nature was socially more influential than nurture.' As a part of this project, 'Neubauer conceived the experiment to compare the development of separated sets of twins and triplets with fellow psychiatrist Viola Bernard to explore whether human behavior is more affected by environment or genetics' (https://bit.ly/3x0Vd5f). The practice went on from the 1940s and only ended in the State of New York in 1980. For further information on this experimenting with human lives, I would highly recommend that you view two documentaries: "The Twinning Reaction" by Lori Shinseki and "Three identical strangers," by Charlotte Hu.

Rhetorical questions: As Africana scholars living in academically liberated zones, what is the objective of your research work and search for knowledge? In whose service are your teaching, research work and publications? Do your conference papers offer any Africana knowledge at the round table of ideas? Is the knowledge you produce liberating and humanizing, or is it for the advancement of your careerist ambition? Do you practice what Professor Nancy Cantor would call "scholarship in action?"[12]

By recognizing the world as one mammoth family of human beings, *utu/ubuntu* maintains that true knowledge should

12 Nancy Cantor was my Chancellor at Syracuse University. She was the first female chancellor to be inaugurated at Syracuse University (2004-2013). "Under her leadership, the University launched *Scholarship in Action* – a vision that challenges higher education institutions to engage all corners of their communities" (https://en.wikipedia.org/wiki/Nancy_Cantor).

not only enhance cross-cultural conversations, but should also ultimately aim at humanizing us. This is what our scholarship should aim at. Our research, scholarship and search for knowledge should take us to as many sites of knowledge as possible even if this might mean moving out of our comfort zones. *Utu/ ubuntu* urges us to move beyond ourselves and to transcend our comfort zones because other people, their experiences and sites of knowledge are a part of who we are; just as we are a part of who they are. So, then, if we are to claim the name of *utu/ubuntu-rooted* transformational scholars, we must allow ideas to argue; to debate; to converse... and yes, let us even allow them to stand in contestation with each other – not out of antagonistic differences or negative competition; but rather, for the sake of heightening debate. If there is no agreement at the end of our debates, then let us cordially agree to disagree without creating what I call a "war zone of ideas."

ENGENDERING OUR WORK, TEACHING AND APPLYING FEMINISM TO OUR WORK

The other very important area that we need to keep challenging ourselves about in Africana Studies and Research is the extent to which we engender our discourses and the priority to which we place upon the application and incorporation of feminism and feminist theory into our curriculum, research and publications. By denouncing patriarchy and speaking/researching/teaching/writing against the oppression, repression, dehumanization, abuse, subjugation, silencing and marginalization of women, we will be going along way towards becoming *utu/ubuntu-rooted* transformational scholars. Equally important, we must recognize that the incorporation of and teaching of/researching on gender and feminism is our collective work and not the responsibility of our female colleagues alone. In teaming up as colleagues to advance studies in feminism, we will be practicing *utu/ubuntu-rooted* transformational scholarship.

Related to feminism is the question of gender inequity and inequality. Mainstream academy has been notorious and sadly backward in dealing with discrimination of women when it comes to job opportunities, pay, promotion and leadership. Most unfortunately, we have not done that much better in Black Studies, especially in terms of women's leadership. If we claim to be *utu/ubuntu-rooted* transformational scholars, let us look unflinchingly in the mirror of truth and ask ourselves questions like: Do we offer jobs to men more readily than to women? Do women earn less than their male counterparts? Where are the women, as chairs or directors of Black Studies programs, departments and centers? Where are they in top administrative levels? The task of breaking the silences behind these questions is more urgent than ever if we are to claim the title of transformational scholars rooted in *utu/ubuntu.*

STUDIES OF THE MARGINALIZED

The foregoing argument applies to the studies of the marginalized, underserved and oppressed in our societies, including: the working masses; people with disability; people of different sexual orientation; transgender people, etc. Having successfully broken through the iron gates of predominantly White academia, Black Studies are obligated to bring along with them other neglected areas of study and to give them space to thrive. The accelerated evolution of curricula, teaching, research and publication highlighting these experiences is important, especially in these times when in America and other parts of the Western world, White supremacists victimize, demonize and terrorize minority groups in the supposed name of nationalism, "civilization" and Christianity. These studies are a part and parcel of *utu/ubuntu-rooted* transformational scholarship.

Through engagement in *utu/ubuntu-rooted* transformational scholarship, Africana Studies and Research will be doing nothing less than 'restoring the soul' of the academy, to borrow a term from President Joe Biden who evokes the need to 'restore the soul of America' in his quest to move the nation beyond Donald Trump's White supremacist, heartless politics of terror, specifically aimed at Blacks, people of color in general, followers of Islam, immigrants of color and other minorities. In my view, without a heart and "soul," education can never be transformative. This is the basic argument that I make in an already referenced book of selected essays and speeches, published by

Professor Kassahun of the African World Press, entitled *Writing and Speaking from the Heart of My Mind*.[13] I fervently believe that transformational scholarship should refrain from preoccupation with theoretical abstraction and instead fiercely engage in *utu/ubuntu-charged* production and dissemination of knowledge. In this regard, I ask my fellow academicians: as Africana scholars, do our studies and research have a heart? How "soulful" and humanizing are our efforts in teaching and research? Is the knowledge we are generating doing anything to transform the world?

That said, I know that in today's academy, utu/ubuntu transformational scholarship often comes at a price, especially during tenure and promotion, as well as when seeking appointments in high academic positions. Indeed, I am aware that in mainstream academy, one has to know how to play the game and, trust me, *utu/ubuntu* transformational scholarship is not the best of chips in this game. So then, the ultimate and decisive question becomes: are we ready as Black studies scholars to pay the price for practicing *utu/ubuntu* transformational scholarship?

13 Mĩcere Gĩthae Mũgo, *ibid.*, 2012.

GUARDIANSHIP OF BLACK STUDIES

The final thing I wish to briefly address is the guardianship of Black Studies.

From their founding, Black Studies programs, departments and centers were never at the top of funding, especially in White, or predominantly-White universities. Like our people, when it comes to funding, those of us in Black studies who are stationed in mainstream academy generally live in very poor neighborhoods – ironically, sometimes physically on the periphery of our campuses. Whenever budgets become tight, mainstream academy looks for every way possible to either abolish, or phase out Black Studies departments. At best, they are made a part of some other department, college, or school. Excuses for these actions abound. Not so long ago, the most popular rationalization for either phasing out or amalgamating Black studies with some other entity was that the field had been overtaken by developments such as Multicultural studies. The underlying argument here is that Multicultural Studies cancel the need for Black Studies. Needless to say, this argument is preposterous, ignorant and false. The truth is that some people in academia have never accepted Black Studies as a valid site of knowledge and so, whenever downsizing is needed, Black studies are the first casualty.

This is something that Africana Studies and Research Center (ASRC) at Cornell knows about. In 2011, or thereabouts, I believe, the center was stripped of the autonomy it had enjoyed since its founding and amalgamated into the College of Arts and Sciences as a kind of department. The decision held, despite protests from students, some faculty, alumni and many colleagues in the Black Studies field all over America and beyond. ASRC is now a mere entity in the College of Arts and Sciences at Cornell University. As we celebrate the 50th anniversary of ASRC, let us remember that the center was founded at great cost. Indeed, we stand on the soil of a zone that was liberated through blood, sweat, tears and struggle. Let us, therefore, ask ourselves: What kind of guardians are we/have we been? Are we careerists and academic merchants that are only interested in our personal academic success even if it is at the cost of Africana? Are we planters, or harvesters who visit the field only at harvest time? Once we are gone, shall we leave firm footprints on this liberated zone, like our forebearers, as evidence that we were here once upon a time as guardians and carriers of this tradition of struggle? These are rhetorical questions, but they challenge us to remember that: This is why and how Black Studies as an academic field was born. This is why and how the Africana Studies and Research Center at Cornell University was born. Today, in celebrating Africana as a liberated academic zone, let us say Asé!

As I come to the end of our conversation, allow me to reiterate that in my view, scholarship is not complete if it is not applied to the reality around us with a view to tackling and if possible, solving the problems that hinder human growth and development. This is the kind of scholarship that Paulo Freire, the late Brazilian educational thinker and activist, referred to as dialogical education for problem solving. This is the kind of education that Black Studies envisaged from the very start: an education that, among other things, sought to address the needs and problems of the communities around the academy, as well as those of global humanity at large. Friends, today the application of knowledge for public good is not just critical, but mandatory. We should, therefore, rid our scholarship of abstraction, mystification, empty theorizing and the terror of lofty, alienating discourse and instead use it to humanize ourselves and the world at large. I therefore request, as I have done many times before, that we bring down our books from the shelves and actively engage in the urgent task of translating the theories they encase into social action that creates growth in and hope for humankind. I believe that commitment to *utu/ubuntu-rooted* scholarship will see us achieve this important goal.

In concluding, let me remind all of us that through our research and scholarship, we are, above all, enhancing and enriching our classroom teaching. Thus, Black/ Africana studies must never relegate teaching to second place in our academic work. Teaching, research, publication and application of knowledge are threaded together such that separating them would dismantle the integrity of the whole. Indeed, any attempt to separate them is doomed to failure because the connectedness of their interlacing composite layers will automatically resist dismantling. A good teacher combines and fuses into one connected whole: research, publication and application of knowledge. We also do well to remember that although a mentor, the teacher/ professor as the transmitter of knowledge, is supposed to be a companion to the learner along the journey of knowledge-acquisition, as opposed to being an "overseer" of sorts. The process of learning is a reciprocal and shared mission, even as the teacher plays the role of mentor, guide and moderator. Thus, in relating to the learners, *utu/ubuntu–rooted* Africana scholars might consider adopting the vision that the late Njeri Kũi Gĩthae-Mũgo articulated so passionately, poetically and powerfully in her doctoral dissertation proposal:

> *In the deepest of places within the person of each child, there is a kernel of genius just sitting there waiting to be let loose to enter the world of learning, discovery, self-discovery, collective discovery and celebration of the multifarious*

gifts that life so generously gives. [As teachers and scholars] let us become agents in unleashing that genius and not inhibiters holding it prisoner. Let us become partners along the journey of learning (be Mwalimus): learning, discovering, faltering and even falling; but getting up and continuing on the journey relentlessly, lifting one another in order to climb to the summit of the mountain of knowledge.[14]

Sober and fitting words indeed to end with, from a graduate alumna of the Africana Studies and Research Center at Cornell, reminding us that student-centered education should occupy a central place in the journey of knowledge production, acquisition, dissemination and application.

Last word: if we are to truly celebrate this 50th anniversary of the Africana Studies and Research Center at Cornell as a milestone in Black studies and if we are to honestly claim that the Center is a liberated zone in academia, then *utu/ubuntu-rooted* scholarship is not an option; but an imperative. Indeed, I believe: This is why and how Black Studies as an academic field was born. This is why and how the Africana Studies and Research Center at Cornell University was born. Today, in celebrating Africana as a liberated academic zone, let us say Asé!

Thank you very much again for giving me this unique honor to hold dialogue with our distinguished audience, in commemoration of Africana's golden anniversary.

14 Quoted from Njeri Gĩthae-Mũgo, "Youth/Child Education, Rights and Participation; Social Justice/ Equality and Human Rights," unpublished doctoral thesis proposal, first draft, 2010.

ABOUT MÎCERE GÎTHAE MŨGO

Mĩcere M. Gĩthae Mũgo, Ph.D. Emerita Professor
Dept. of African American Studies, Syracuse University.

Mîcere Gîthae Mũgo is a poet, playwright, literary critic and Emerita Full Professor, retired from the Department of African American Studies at Syracuse University in May 2015. A Kenyan by birth, she has two daughters, Mũmbi and the late Njeri, whom she describes as her "comrades" and close friends.

Dr. Mũgo has been in the teaching profession since 1967 and has served in such distinguished positions as: high school headmistress, university department/unit head, first woman faculty dean at the University of Nairobi in 1980, East African Examinations Council's first Chief Examiner of English and Literature, etc. Prof. Mũgo joined the Department of African American Studies, Syracuse University, in 1993 and during her tenure served as Director of Graduate Studies, Chair of the SU-wide Africa Initiative and from 2005-8, as Chair of the Department. In the late 1990s she served as the Director of SU DIPA's Summer Traveling

Seminar to Southern Africa while across SU she has served on: the University Senate, its subcommittees, the Chancellor's Citation Awards Committee, the Faculty Council, the College Academic Committee, the Honors Program's Board, the DIPA Program Committee, the Humanities Council and a host of others.

During her tenure at Syracuse University, Dr. Mũgo received no less than 25 awards for teaching, advising, academic excellence and community service from students' organizations; Syracuse University; and the Syracuse Community at large.

In December 2020 she was awarded a Doctor of Letters honorary degree from the University of Nairobi. In December 2013, she was awarded the Elder of the Burning Spear and in 2012, the Mwalimu Julius Nyerere Distinguished Lecturer Award. In 2008 she received the CNY Women of Distinction Award and in 2007, the academic Distinguished Africanist Award, while in 2004 she was named Laura J. and L. Douglas Meredith Professor for Teaching Excellence, becoming the first Black person at SU to receive this honor. In Kenya, The East African Standard Century publication of November 2002 cited her among "The Top 100: They Influenced Kenya Most" during the 20th Century list. Mũgo's publications include 6 books, 1 co-authored play, 8 co-edited supplementary readers for Zimbabwean schools and an edited journal, Third World in Perspective. She has many chapters in various books, 4 monographs, a lot of internationally anthologized poems, numerous reviews, interviews and citations.

During her stay in Syracuse, Dr. Mũgo's community activism has involved volunteer work in Central New York prisons; among refugees, including Board membership on the D.C. based African International Refugee Foundation; Inter-Faith Works of CNY; the "Free Mumia" campaign; anti-war campaigns; debt cancellation mobilization against the World Bank and IMF; Amnesty International work; numerous human rights projects – nationally and internationally – especially with regard to women and children. Professor Mũgo is a member of the Ghana Society of

Central New York and a founder of the Pan African Community of Central New York, which she has presided over twice since the organization's founding. She is also the founder of the Syracuse community-based United Women of Africa Organization and its former President. On the SU campus she was instrumental to the designing of the M.A. in Pan African Studies within the Department of African American Studies.

Professor Mũgo has served on the board of directors of many international organizations and on equally many editorial boards. A committed community activist, Mĩcere Gĩthae Mũgo is a passionate advocate for human rights especially as they have historically been denied to Blacks, women, children, the masses and other marginalized groups internationally. She is a highly sought-after public speaker.

L - #0238 - 040821 - C39 - 229/152/2 - PB - DID3139534

It is hard not to be effusive about the author of this pamphlet. Let's just say it loud: Mĩcere Gĩthae Mũgo is a legend in her own time. And ours. Ours because, as she would say, paraphrasing universal African wisdom: without us, there is no her. From her native Kenya, a source to which she returns continually for yet more ancient wisdom; to Zimbabwe, where she once found refuge on being forced to flee her native land in the face of political persecution; to the United States of America, to which she eventually emigrated; and beyond, way beyond, Professor Comrade Sister Mugo has been a lodestar and wonder—in the academy and in the community, locally and globally.

This pamphlet is a discursive offering to Africana studies, a notebook on a field of study born of struggle, student-led struggle. The organizing principle is **Utu-Ubuntu**, the universal African moral conception centered on the paramountcy of the soul over material accumulation. It is a stinging rebuke to capitalism, imperialism, racism, sexism, heterosexism and all the other antihuman isms, Utu-Ubuntu. Here, indeed, is an Africana studies manifesto, one that should be required reading for all students of the field, in and out of the academy.

She never ceases to educate, to enlighten, to energize—this soul sister, this scion of Utu-Ubuntu, this magnificent struggler in the cause of African vindication and human liberation, Mĩcere Gĩthae Mũgo.

— **Michael O. West**, Professor of African American Studies; History; African Studies, Penn State University

An insightful essay that insists that Africana research and scholarship has "to have both mind and heart" to be truly emancipatory—for that is the essence of the meaning of Ubuntu and of Utu, the Swahili equivalent. That is the basis for challenging the dominant colonizing cultures that seek to dehumanize our people. The inimitable Mĩcere Mũgo forces us to think about the purpose of teaching and research: whose interests do they serve?

— **Dr. Willy Mutunga**, Chief Justice & President of Supreme Court, Republic of Kenya, 2011-2016

An excellent celebration of the contribution of Utu/Ubuntu—African Indigenous Knowledge—to Africana scholarship by Professor Mĩcere Mũgo, an icon of Africana Studies. This epistemological imperative for the creation of 'liberated academic zones' advances the post-modern and critical theory traditions, while firmly establishing Africa's unique contributions, not only to Africana Scholarship, but also to the Global Academy and to humanity.

— **Filomina Chioma Steady**, D.Phil. (Oxon.)
Professor Emerita and Former Chair, Africana Studies, Wellesley College